The most wonderful stuff!

The most wonderful stuff!

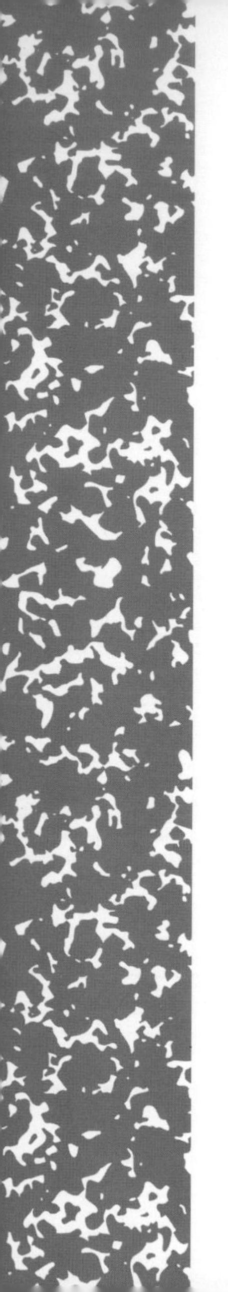

Published in the United States by Random House Children's Books,
a division of Penguin Random House LLC, New York.
The artwork that appears herein was first published in various books by Dr. Seuss.

Random House and the colophon are registered trademarks of Penguin Random House LLC.

Visit us on the Web!
Seussville.com
rhcbooks.com

Educators and librarians, for a variety of teaching tools, visit us at
RHTeachersLibrarians.com

ISBN 978-0-593-38119-9 (hardcover)

MANUFACTURED IN CHINA 10 9 8 7 6 5 4 3 2 1 First Edition

Random House Children's Books supports the First Amendment
and celebrates the right to read.

Dr. Seuss's

OH, WHAT I'VE

LEARNED

Thanks to My TEACHERS!

Random House New York

Oh, what
I've learned
because of my
TEACHERS!

From my ABCs . . .

ABCDEFGHIJKLMN
OPQRSTUVWXY
Z
O

to my **123**s.

76528 804927
9
637
4932
670
6
094014

From the **HISTORY** of our world . . .

to **FACTS** about worlds that are far away.

Thanks to my teachers,
I've learned the joys
of making **MUSIC**
and **ART** . . .

the importance of
PHYSICAL FITNESS . . .

and the pleasure of READING a good book.

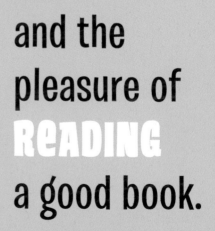

Thanks to my teachers,
I've learned to **SHARE** . . .

and to **HELP** others.

I've learned how to work as part of a **TEAM** . . .

and that sometimes
I need to find
my **OWN WAY**.

Because of my **TEACHERS**,
I can move mountains!

THANK YOU for
all that you do.

Oh, the stuff I have learned!

Oh, the stuff I have learned!

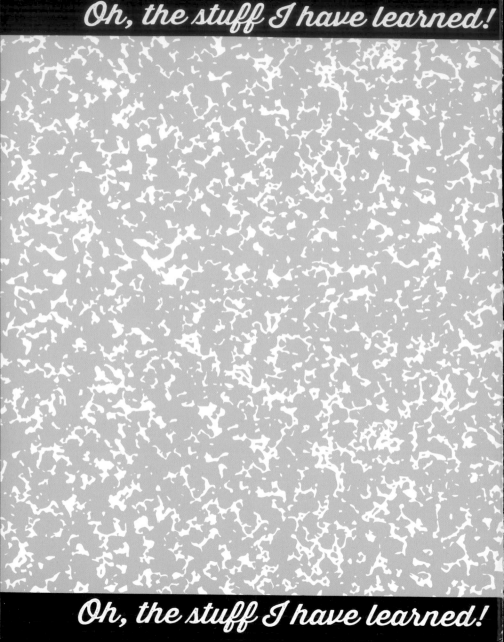